UNCERTAIN TIMES, UNFAILING PROMISES:

Trusting God in an Anxious Age

SMITH FREEMAN
Publishing

Uncertain Times, Unfailing Promises: Trusing God in an Anxious Age

Bible verses were taken from the following translations:

Scripture quotations marked HCSB are taken from the Holman Christian Standard Bible®, Used by Permission HCSB © 1999, 2000, 2002, 2003, 2009 Holman Bible Publishers. Holman Christian Standard Bible®, Holman CSB®, and HCSB® are federally registered trademarks of Holman Bible Publishers.

Scripture quotations marked (KJV) are from the King James Version. Public domain.

Scripture quotations marked MSG are taken from *THE MESSAGE*, copyright © 1993, 2002, 2018 by Eugene H. Peterson. Used by permission of NavPress. All rights reserved. Represented by Tyndale House Publishers, a Division of Tyndale House Ministries.

Scripture quotations marked (NASB) are from the New American Standard Bible® (NASB), Copyright © 1960, 1962, 1963,1968, 1971, 1972, 1973, 1975, 1977, 1995 by The Lockman Foundation. Used by permission. www.Lockman.org.

Scripture quotations marked (NCV) are taken from the New Century Version®. Copyright © 2005 by Thomas Nelson. Used by permission. All rights reserved.

Scripture quotations marked (NIV) are taken from the Holy Bible, New International Version®, NIV®. Copyright © 1973, 1978, 1984, 2011 by Biblica, Inc.™ Used by permission of Zondervan. All rights reserved worldwide. www.zondervan.com The "NIV" and "New International Version" are trademarks registered in the United States Patent and Trademark Office by Biblica, Inc.™

Scripture quotations marked (NKJV) are taken from the New King James Version®. Copyright © 1982 by Thomas Nelson. Used by permission. All rights reserved.

Scripture quotations marked (NLT) are taken from the Holy Bible, New Living Translation, copyright © 1996, 2004, 2015 by Tyndale House Foundation. Used by permission of Tyndale House Publishers, a Division of Tyndale House Ministries, Carol Stream, Illinois 60188. All rights reserved.

Cover design by Kim Russell | Wahoo Designs

ISBN: 979-8-9872584-0-8

A MESSAGE TO READERS

We know that all things work together for the good of those who love God: those who are called according to His purpose.

ROMANS 8:28 HCSB

God's Word promises that all things work together for the good of those who love Him. Yet sometimes, when we encounter troubling circumstances or uncertain times, we simply cannot comprehend how those events might be a part of God's plan for our lives. We experience pain or adversity, and we honestly wonder if recovery is possible. But with God, all things are possible.

The Christian faith, as communicated through the words of the Holy Bible, is a healing faith. It offers comfort in times of uncertainty and hope instead of hopelessness. Through the healing words of God's promises, we are taught that the Lord continues to manifest His plans through good times and hard times.

This book contains thirty Bible promises that every Christian should trust and live by. The ideas in these chapters are intended to serve as powerful reminders: reminders of God's commandments, reminders of God's promises, reminders of God's gifts, and reminders of God's love.

These are uncertain times, difficult times for many of us. Yet adversity is not meant to be feared, it is meant to be worked through. If this text assists you, even in a small way, as you move through and beyond your own uncertainties and doubts, it will have served its purpose. May God bless you and keep you today, tomorrow, and forever.

As for God, His way is perfect;
the word of the Lord is proven;
He is a shield to all who trust in Him.

PSALM 18:30 NKJV

1

GOD ALWAYS KEEPS HIS PROMISES

Let us hold on to the confession of our hope
without wavering, for He who promised is faithful.

HEBREWS 10:23 HCSB

The Bible contains promises upon which you, as a believer, can depend. When the Creator of the universe makes a pledge to you, He keeps it. No exceptions. In fact, you can think of the Bible as a written contract between you and your heavenly Father. When you fulfill your obligations to Him, the Lord will most certainly fulfill His covenant to you.

When we welcome Christ into our hearts, God promises us the opportunity to experience contentment, peace, and spiritual abundance. But more importantly, God promises that the priceless gift of eternal life will be ours. These promises should give us comfort because, with God on our side, we have absolutely nothing to fear in this world and everything to hope for in the next.

Are you concerned about these uncertain times? Be comforted and trust the promises that God has made to you. Are you worried or anxious? Be confident in God's power. Are you confused? Listen to the quiet voice of your heavenly Father. He is not a God of confusion. Talk with Him; listen to Him; trust Him, and trust His promises. He is steadfast, and He is your protector today, tomorrow, and every day after that.

MORE THOUGHTS ABOUT GOD'S PROMISES

There are four words I wish we would never
forget, and they are, "God keeps his word."

CHARLES SWINDOLL

The stars may fall, but God's promises
will stand and be fulfilled.

J. I. PACKER

We honor God by asking for great things when they are a part
of His promise. We dishonor Him and cheat ourselves when
we ask for molehills where He has promised mountains.

VANCE HAVNER

The promises of Scripture are not mere pious hopes
or sanctified guesses. They are more than sentimental
words to be printed on decorated cards for Sunday
School children. They are eternal verities. They
are true. There is no perhaps about them.

PETER MARSHALL

Gather the riches of God's promises. Nobody
can take away from you those texts from the
Bible which you have learned by heart.

CORRIE TEN BOOM

MORE FROM GOD'S WORD

*Sustain me as You promised, and I will live; do
not let me be ashamed of my hope.*

PSALM 119:116 HCSB

*They will bind themselves to the LORD with an eternal
covenant that will never again be forgotten.*

JEREMIAH 50:5 NLT

*My God is my rock, in whom I take refuge, my
shield and the horn of my salvation.*

2 SAMUEL 22:2–3 NIV

He heeded their prayer, because they put their trust in him.

1 CHRONICLES 5:20 NKJV

*Teach me to do Your will, for You are my God; Your
Spirit is good. Lead me in the land of uprightness.*

PSALM 143:10 NKJV

A TIMELY TIP

Today, spend time thinking about the role that God's Word plays
in your life. And while you're at it, ask the Lord for the wisdom to
worry less and to trust Him more.

2

THE PROMISE: WHEN YOU TRUST THE LORD, HE WILL LEAD YOU THROUGH UNCERTAIN TIMES

Trust in the LORD with all your heart, and lean not on your own understanding; in all your ways acknowledge Him, and He shall direct your paths.

PROVERBS 3:5-6 NKJV

As we pass through this world, we travel past emotional peaks and valleys. When we reach the mountaintops of life, we find it easy to praise our Creator. And as we reach the crest of the mountain's peak, we find it easy to trust His plan. But when we find ourselves in the darker valleys of life—when we face uncertainty, disappointment, or despair—we may find it more difficult to trust our heavenly Father. Yet trust Him we must.

As Christians, we can be comforted: whether we find ourselves at the pinnacle of the mountain or the darkest depths of the valley, God is there. And we Christians have every reason to live courageously. After all, Christ has already won the ultimate battle on the cross at Calvary.

So the next time you find your courage tested to the limit, lean upon God's promises. Trust His Son. Remember that the Lord is always near and that He is on your side. When you are worried, anxious, or afraid, call upon Him. God can handle your problems infinitely better than you can, so turn them over to Him. Remember that the Lord rules both mountaintops and valleys—with limitless wisdom and love—now and forever.

MORE THOUGHTS ABOUT TRUSTING GOD

When a train goes through a tunnel and it gets dark, you don't throw away your ticket and jump off. You sit still and trust the engineer.

CORRIE TEN BOOM

One of the marks of spiritual maturity is the quiet confidence that God is in control, without the need to understand why he does what he does.

CHARLES SWINDOLL

Faith and obedience are bound up in the same bundle. He that obeys God, trusts God; and he that trusts God, obeys God.

C. H. SPURGEON

Never be afraid to trust an unknown future to a known God.

CORRIE TEN BOOM

Never yield to gloomy anticipation. Place your hope and confidence in God. He has no record of failure.

LETTIE COWMAN

MORE FROM GOD'S WORD

In quietness and trust is your strength.

ISAIAH 30:15 NASB

The LORD is my rock, my fortress, and my deliverer, my God, my mountain where I seek refuge. My shield, the horn of my salvation, my stronghold, my refuge, and my Savior.

2 SAMUEL 22:2–3 HCSB

The fear of man is a snare, but the one who trusts in the LORD is protected.

PROVERBS 29:25 HCSB

Those who trust in the LORD are like Mount Zion. It cannot be shaken; it remains forever.

PSALM 125:1 HCSB

Jesus said, "Don't let your hearts be troubled. Trust in God, and trust in me."

JOHN 14:1 NCV

REMEMBER THIS

Because God is trustworthy—and because He has made promises to you that He intends to keep—you are protected. The Lord always keeps His promises. Trust Him.

3

THE PROMISE: WHEN YOU PUT GOD FIRST, HE WILL PROVIDE FOR YOUR NEEDS

*But seek first the kingdom of God and His righteousness,
and all these things will be provided for you.*

MATTHEW 6:33 HCSB

When uncertain times arrive, as they do from time to time, pressures begin to mount. We have an assortment of things to worry about and a long list of obligations at home, at work, and many places in between. From the moment we rise until we the moment we drift off to sleep at night, we have things to do and things to think about. So how do we find time for God? We must *make* time for Him, plain and simple. When we put God first, we're blessed. But when we succumb to the pressures and distractions of everyday life, we inevitably pay a price for our misguided priorities.

In the book of Exodus, God warns that we should put no gods before Him. Yet all too often, we place our Lord in second, third, or fourth place as we focus on other things. When we place our desires for possessions and status above our obligations to Him—or when we yield to the countless distractions that surround us—we forfeit the peace that might otherwise be ours.

In the wilderness, Satan offered Jesus earthly power and unimaginable riches, but Jesus refused. Instead, He chose to worship His heavenly Father. We must do likewise by putting God first and worshiping Him only. God must come first. Always first.

MORE THOUGHTS ABOUT PUTTING GOD FIRST

We become whatever we are committed to.

RICK WARREN

Worship in the truest sense
takes place only when our full
attention is on God—His glory,
majesty, love, and compassion.

BILLY GRAHAM

Put your trust in God
and go calmly on your way.

NORMAN VINCENT PEALE

When all else is gone, God is still left.
Nothing changes Him.

HANNAH WHITALL SMITH

To God be the glory,
great things He has done;
So loved He the world
that He gave us His Son.

FANNY CROSBY

MORE FROM GOD'S WORD

You shall have no other gods before Me.

EXODUS 20:3 NKJV

*Therefore, whether you eat or drink,
or whatever you do, do all to the glory of God.*

1 CORINTHIANS 10:31 NKJV

*For this is the love of God, that we keep His commandments.
And His commandments are not burdensome.*

1 JOHN 5:3 NKJV

How happy is everyone who fears the LORD, who walks in His ways!

PSALM 128:1 HCSB

*But prove yourselves doers of the word, and not
merely hearers who delude themselves.*

JAMES 1:22 NASB

A TIMELY TIP

Think about your priorities. Are you *really* putting God first in your life, or are you putting other things—things like material possessions or personal status—ahead of your relationship with Him? If, after careful consideration, you determine that your priorities have become somewhat misaligned, think of at least three things you can do today to put God where He belongs: in first place.

4

THE PROMISE: WHEN YOU CAST YOUR BURDENS ON THE LORD, HE WILL CALM YOUR FEARS

Cast your burden on the LORD, and He shall sustain you;
He shall never permit the righteous to be moved.

PSALM 55:22 NKJV

Because you have the ability to think, you also have the ability to worry. Even if you're a faithful Christian, you may be plagued by occasional periods of discouragement and doubt. Even though you trust God's promise of eternal life—even though you sincerely believe in God's love and protection—you may find yourself upset by uncertain times or difficult circumstances. Jesus understood your concerns when he spoke the reassuring words found in the sixth chapter of Matthew:

Therefore I say to you, do not worry about your life, what you will eat or what you will drink; nor about your body, what you will put on. Is not life more than food and the body more than clothing? Look at the birds of the air, for they neither sow nor reap nor gather into barns; yet your heavenly Father feeds them. Are you not of more value than they? Which of you by worrying can add one cubit to his stature? . . . Therefore do not worry about tomorrow, for tomorrow will worry about its own things. Sufficient for the day is its own trouble. V. 25–27, 34

Where is the best place to take your concerns? Take them to God. Take your troubles to Him; take your fears to Him; take your doubts to Him; take your sorrows to Him . . . and leave them all there. Seek protection from your Creator and build your spiritual house upon the Rock that cannot be moved.

Perhaps you are concerned about your future, your relationships, or your finances. Or perhaps you are simply a worrier by nature. If so, refer to Matthew 6 often. This beautiful passage will remind you that the Lord still sits in His heaven and that you are His beloved child. Then, perhaps, you will worry a little less and trust God a little more. And that's as it should be because God is trustworthy, and you are protected.

MORE THOUGHTS ABOUT OVERCOMING WORRY

Much that worries us beforehand can, quite unexpectedly, have a happy and simple solution. Worries just don't matter. Things really are in a better hand than ours.

DIETRICH BONHOEFFER

With the peace of God to guard us and the
God of peace to guide us—why worry?

WARREN WIERSBE

The more you meditate on God's Word, the
less you will have to worry about.

RICK WARREN

Our fears for today, our worries about tomorrow, and
even the powers of hell can't keep God's love away.

BILL BRIGHT

MORE FROM GOD'S WORD

*Let not your heart be troubled; you believe
in God, believe also in Me.*

JOHN 14:1 NKJV

Cast all your anxiety on him because he cares for you.

1 PETER 5:7 NIV

*Do not be anxious about anything, but in every situation, by prayer
and petition, with thanksgiving, present your requests to God.*

PHILIPPIANS 4:6 NIV

*Let us hold tightly without wavering to the hope we
affirm, for God can be trusted to keep his promise.*

HEBREWS 10:23 NLT

A TIMELY TIP

Assiduously divide your areas of concern into two categories: those
you can change and those you cannot. Resolve never to waste time
or energy worrying about the latter. Focus, instead, on the things
you can change—more specifically, the things you *should* change—
and get busy changing them.

5

THE PROMISE: THE WORLD CHANGES, BUT GOD DOES NOT

For I am the LORD, I do not change.

MALACHI 3:6 NKJV

Our world is in a state of constant change. God is not. At times, the world seems to be trembling beneath our feet, but we can be comforted in the knowledge that our heavenly Father is the rock that cannot be shaken.

Every day that we live, we mortals encounter a multitude of changes—some good, some not so good, some downright discouraging. And on occasion, all of us must endure life-changing personal losses that leave us breathless. When we do, our loving heavenly Father stands ready to protect us, to comfort us, to guide us, and, in time, to heal us.

Are you facing uncertain times or unwelcome changes? If so, please remember that God is far bigger than any problem you may face. So instead of worrying about life's inevitable challenges, put your faith in the Father and His only begotten Son. Remind yourself that, "Jesus Christ is the same yesterday, today, and forever" (Hebrews 13:8 HCSB). And rest assured: it is precisely because your Savior does not change that you can face your challenges with courage for today and hope for the future.

MORE THOUGHTS ABOUT CHANGE

You can endure change by pondering His permanence.

MAX LUCADO

The only way to keep your balance is to fix your eyes on
the One who never changes. If you gaze too long at your
circumstances, you will become dizzy and confused.

SARAH YOUNG

If you are going through difficult times today,
hold steady. It will change soon.

JAMES DOBSON

If we will only surrender ourselves utterly to the Lord and
will trust Him perfectly, we shall find our souls "mounting up
with wings as eagles" to the "heavenly places" in Christ Jesus,
where earthly annoyances have no power to disturb us.

HANNAH WHITALL SMITH

MORE FROM GOD'S WORD

*The LORD says, "Forget what happened before, and do
not think about the past. Look at the new thing I am going
to do. It is already happening. Don't you see it? I will
make a road in the desert and rivers in the dry land."*

ISAIAH 43:18–19 NCV

*There is a time for everything, and a season
for every activity under heaven.*

ECCLESIASTES 3:1 NIV

*The wise see danger ahead and avoid it, but
fools keep going and get into trouble.*

PROVERBS 27:12 NCV

*You are being renewed in the spirit of your minds; you
put on the new self, the one created according to God's
likeness in righteousness and purity of the truth.*

EPHESIANS 4:23–24 HCSB

In quietness and trust is your strength.

ISAIAH 30:15 NASB

REMEMBER THIS

Change is inevitable; growth is not. God will come to your doorstep on countless occasions with opportunities to learn and to grow. And He will knock. Your challenge, of course, is to open the door and answer. So the next time you're faced with an opportunity disguised as an unwelcome change, ask yourself this question: "What does God want me to do?" Then act accordingly.

6

THE PROMISE: WHEN TIMES ARE TOUGH, THE LORD CAN HEAL YOUR HEART

He heals the brokenhearted and binds up their wounds.

PSALM 147:3 HCSB

All of us encounter occasional disappointments and setbacks. None of us are exempt. When tough times arrive, we may be forced to rearrange our plans and our priorities, but even on our darkest days, we must remember that God's love remains constant. And we must never forget that God intends for us to use our setbacks as stepping-stones on the path to a better life.

The fact that we encounter adversity is not nearly so important as the way we choose to deal with it. When tough times arrive, we have a clear choice: we can begin the difficult work of tackling our troubles, or not. When we summon the courage to look Old Man Trouble squarely in the eye, he usually blinks. But if we refuse to address our problems, even the smallest annoyances have a way of growing into king-sized catastrophes.

Psalm 145 promises, "The Lord is near to all who call on him, to all who call on him in truth. He fulfills the desires of those who fear him; he hears their cry and saves them" (vv. 18–19 NIV). And the words of Jesus offer us comfort: "These things I have spoken to you, that in Me you may have peace. In the world you will have tribulation; but be of good cheer, I have overcome the world" (John 16:33 NKJV).

As believers, we know that God loves us and that He will protect us. During uncertain times, He comforts us; in times of sorrow, He dries our tears. When we are troubled, or weak, or sorrowful, the Lord is always with us. We must trust Him and take comfort in His promises. And then we must begin the difficult work of tackling our problems because if we don't, who will? Or should?

MORE THOUGHTS ABOUT DEALING WITH DIFFICULT TIMES

Often the trials we mourn are really gateways
into the good things we long for.

HANNAH WHITALL SMITH

Jesus does not say, "There is no storm."
He says "I am here, do not toss, but trust."

VANCE HAVNER

As we wait on God, He helps us use
the winds of adversity to soar above our problems.
As the Bible says, "Those who wait on the LORD . . .
shall mount up with wings like eagles."

BILLY GRAHAM

If God sends us on stony paths,
he provides strong shoes.

CORRIE TEN BOOM

MORE FROM GOD'S WORD

We are hard-pressed on every side, yet not crushed;
we are perplexed, but not in despair.

2 Corinthians 4:8 NKJV

I called to the LORD in my distress; I called to my
God. From His temple He heard my voice.

2 Samuel 22:7 HCSB

The LORD is my rock, my fortress, and my deliverer, my God,
my mountain where I seek refuge. My shield, the horn of
my salvation, my stronghold, my refuge, and my Savior.

2 Samuel 22:2–3 HCSB

God blesses those who patiently endure testing and
temptation. Afterward they will receive the crown of
life that God has promised to those who love him.

James 1:12 NLT

A TIMELY TIP

If you're having tough times, don't hit the panic button and don't keep everything bottled up inside. Instead, talk things over with people you trust. A second opinion (or, for that matter, a third, fourth, or fifth opinion) is usually helpful. So if your troubles seem overwhelming, be willing to seek outside help, starting, of course, with your pastor.

7

THE PROMISE: YOU CAN PRAY CONFIDENTLY

The earnest prayer of a righteous person has great power and produces wonderful results.

JAMES 5:16 NLT

God promises that your prayers are powerful. God promises that He answers prayer (although His answers are not always in accordance with our desires). God invites us to be still and to feel His presence. So pray. Pray about matters great and small; and be watchful for the answers that God most assuredly sends your way.

Is prayer an integral part of your daily life or is it a hit-or-miss routine? Do you "pray without ceasing," or is your prayer life an afterthought? Do you carve out quiet moments with your Creator, or do you bow your head only when others are watching? As you answer those questions, remember that the quality of your spiritual life will be in direct proportion to the quality of your prayer life.

Prayer changes things, and it changes you. So today, instead of turning things over in your mind, turn them over to the Lord in prayer. Instead of worrying about your next decision, ask God for answers. Don't limit your prayers to meals or to bedtime; pray constantly and confidently. God is listening; He wants to hear from you; and you most certainly need to hear from Him.

MORE THOUGHTS ABOUT PRAYER

Prayer is not a work that can be
allocated to one or another group
in the church. It is everybody's
responsibility; it is everybody's privilege.

A. W. TOZER

Prayer connects us with
God's limitless potential.

HENRY BLACKABY

God shapes the world by prayer.
The more praying there is in the world,
the better the world will be, and
the mightier will be the forces against evil.

E. M. BOUNDS

Prayer shouldn't be casual or sporadic,
dictated only by the needs of the moment.
Prayer should be as much a
apart of our lives as breathing.

BILLY GRAHAM

I have found the perfect antidote
for fear. Whenever it sticks up its
ugly face, I clobber it with prayer.

DALE EVANS ROGERS

MORE FROM GOD'S WORD

Rejoice always, pray without ceasing, in everything give thanks; for this is the will of God in Christ Jesus for you.

1 THESSALONIANS 5:16–18 NKJV

Anyone who is having troubles should pray.

JAMES 5:13 NCV

I desire therefore that the men pray everywhere, lifting up holy hands, without wrath and doubting.

1 TIMOTHY 2:8 NKJV

Don't worry about anything, but in everything, through prayer and petition with thanksgiving, let your requests be made known to God.

PHILIPPIANS 4:6 HCSB

The LORD is far from the wicked, but he hears the prayer of the righteous.

PROVERBS 15:29 NIV

A TIMELY TIP

Prayer is always necessary, but it's absolutely essential during difficult times. Martin Luther observed, "If I should neglect prayer but a single day, I should lose a great deal of the fire of faith." Those words apply to you too. And it's up to you to live—and to pray—accordingly.

8

THE PROMISE: THE LORD IS IN CONTROL

He is the Lord. He will do what He thinks is good.

1 SAMUEL 3:18 HCSB

If you're like most people, you like being in control. Period. You want things to happen according to your wishes and according to your timetable. But sometimes, God has other plans . . . and He always has the final word.

Oswald Chambers correctly observed, "Our Lord never asks us to decide for Him; He asks us to yield to Him—a very different matter." These words remind us that even when we cannot understand our heavenly Father's intricate plans, we must trust Him and accept His will.

When Jesus went to the Mount of Olives, as described in Luke 22, He poured out His heart to God. Jesus knew of the agony that He was destined to endure, but He also knew that God's will must be done. We, like our Savior, face trials that bring fear and trembling to the very depths of our souls, but like Christ, we too must ultimately seek God's will, not our own.

Are you embittered by a personal tragedy or by a life-altering disappointment that you did not deserve and cannot fully understand? If so, it's time to make peace with life. It's time to forgive others, and, if necessary, to forgive yourself. It's time to accept the unchangeable past, to embrace the priceless present, and to have faith in the promise of tomorrow. It's time to trust God completely. And it's time to reclaim the peace—His peace—that can and should be yours.

MORE THOUGHTS ABOUT ACCEPTING GOD'S CONTROL

Christians who are strong in the faith grow as they
accept whatever God allows to enter their lives.

BILLY GRAHAM

One of the marks of spiritual maturity is the quiet
confidence that God is in control, without the need
to understand why he does what he does.

CHARLES SWINDOLL

Loving Him means the thankful acceptance of
all things that His love has appointed.

ELISABETH ELLIOT

Accept each day as it comes to you. Do not waste your time
and energy wishing for a different set of circumstances.

SARAH YOUNG

Acceptance says, "True, this is my situation at the moment.
I'll look unblinkingly at the reality of it. But, I'll also open my
hands to accept willingly whatever a loving Father sends."

CATHERINE MARSHALL

MORE FROM GOD'S WORD

*Should we accept only good things from the
hand of God and never anything bad?*

JOB 2:10 NLT

*Everything God made is good, and nothing should
be refused if it is accepted with thanks.*

1 TIMOTHY 4:4 NCV

*Trust in the LORD with all your heart and lean
not on your own understanding.*

PROVERBS 3:5 NIV

*For Yahweh is good, and His love is eternal; His
faithfulness endures through all generations.*

PSALM 100:5 HCSB

*For now we see in a mirror, dimly, but then face to face. Now I
know in part, but then I shall know just as I also am known.*

1 CORINTHIANS 13:12 NKJV

A TIMELY TIP

Acceptance means learning to trust God more. Today, think of at
least one aspect of your life that you've been reluctant to accept.
Then prayerfully ask God to help you trust Him more by accepting
your past and moving on with your life.

9

THE PROMISE: GOD IS CONSTANTLY PROVIDING OPPORTUNITIES FOR RENEWAL AND GROWTH

*Remember ye not the former things, neither consider
the things of old. Behold, I will do a new thing.*

ISAIAH 43:18–19 KJV

As you look at the landscape of your life, do you see opportunities, possibilities, and blessings, or do you focus, instead, upon the more negative scenery? Do you believe the Bible's promise that God is making all things new—including you—or do you believe that it's a promise that applies only to other people? If you've acquired the unfortunate habit of focusing too intently upon the negative aspects of your life, then your spiritual vision is in need of correction.

Whether you realize it or not, opportunities are whirling around you like stars crossing the night sky: beautiful to observe, but too numerous to count. Yet you may be too concerned with the uncertainties of everyday life to notice those opportunities. That's why you should slow down occasionally, catch your breath, and focus your thoughts on two things: the talents God has given you and the opportunities that He has placed before you. The Lord is leading you in the direction of those opportunities. Your task is to watch carefully, to pray fervently, and to act accordingly.

If you're consistently looking for the silver linings instead of

31

the clouds, you'll discover that opportunities have a way of turning up in the most unexpected places. But if you've acquired the unfortunate habit of looking for problems instead of possibilities, you'll find that troubles have a way of turning up in unexpected places too. Since you're likely to find what you're looking for, why not look for opportunities? They're out there. And the rest is up to you.

MORE THOUGHTS ABOUT OPPORTUNITIES

We are all faced with a series of great opportunities
brilliantly disguised as impossible situations.

CHARLES SWINDOLL

Each day is God's gift of a fresh unspoiled
opportunity to live according to His priorities.

ELIZABETH GEORGE

The past is our teacher; the present is our
opportunity; the future is our friend.

EDWIN LOUIS COLE

A possibility is a hint from God.

SØREN KIERKEGAARD

Have thy tools ready; God will find thee work.

CHARLES KINGSLEY

MORE FROM GOD'S WORD

But as it is written: What eye did not see and ear did not hear,
and what never entered the human mind—
God prepared this for those who love Him.

1 Corinthians 2:9 HCSB

Whenever we have the opportunity, we should do good to
everyone,especially to those in the family of faith.

Galatians 6:10 NLT

I can do all things through Christ which strengtheneth me.

Philippians 4:13 KJV

But those who wait on the Lord shall renew their strength;
they shall mount up with wings like eagles, they shall run
and not be weary, they shall walk and not faint.

Isaiah 40:31 NKJV

REMEMBER THIS

God gives us opportunities for a reason: to use them. And He wants you to make the most of the opportunities He sends your way. Billy Graham observed, "Life is a glorious opportunity." That's sound advice, so keep looking for your opportunities and when you find them, take advantage of them sooner rather than later.

10

THE PROMISE: JESUS OFFERS THE ULTIMATE PEACE

The peace of God, which passeth all understanding, shall keep your hearts and minds through Christ Jesus.

PHILIPPIANS 4:7 KJV

Peace. It's such a beautiful word. It conveys images of serenity, contentment, and freedom from the trials and tribulations of everyday existence. Peace means freedom from conflict, freedom from inner turmoil, and freedom from doubt. Peace is such a beautiful concept that advertisers and marketers attempt to sell it with images of relaxed vacationers lounging on the beach or happy senior citizens celebrating "the good life" on the golf course. But contrary to the implied claims of modern media, real peace—genuine peace—isn't for sale. At any price.

Have you discovered the genuine peace that can be yours through Jesus Christ? Or are you still scurrying after the illusion of peace that the world promises but cannot deliver? If you've turned things over to Jesus, you'll be blessed now and forever. So what are you waiting for? Let Him rule your heart and your thoughts, beginning now. When you do, you'll experience the peace that only He can give.

MORE THOUGHTS ABOUT
FINDING PEACE IN DIFFICULT TIMES

Deep within the center of the soul is a chamber of peace
where God lives and where, if we will enter it and quiet
all the other sounds, we can hear His gentle whisper.

LETTIE COWMAN

Peace does not mean to be in a place where there is no
noise, trouble, or hard work. Peace means to be in the
midst of all those things and still be calm in your heart.

CATHERINE MARSHALL

In the center of a hurricane there is absolute quiet and peace.
There is no safer place than in the center of the will of God.

CORRIE TEN BOOM

God's power is great enough for our deepest desperation.
You can go on. You can pick up the pieces and start
anew. You can face your fears. You can find peace
in the rubble. There is healing for your soul.

SUZANNE DALE EZELL

Only Christ can meet the deepest needs of our world
and our hearts. Christ alone can bring lasting peace.

BILLY GRAHAM

MORE FROM GOD'S WORD

Peace I leave with you, My peace I give to you; not as the world gives do I give to you. Let not your heart be troubled, neither let it be afraid.

JOHN 14:27 NKJV

He Himself is our peace.

EPHESIANS 2:14 NASB

But the fruit of the Spirit is love, joy, peace, patience, kindness, goodness, faith, gentleness, self-control. Against such things there is no law.

GALATIANS 5:22–23 HCSB

"I will give peace, real peace, to those far and near, and I will heal them," says the LORD.

ISAIAH 57:19 NCV

These things I have spoken to you, that in Me you may have peace. In the world you will have tribulation; but be of good cheer, I have overcome the world.

JOHN 16:33 NKJV

A TIMELY TIP

God's peace is available to you this very moment *if* you place absolute trust in Him. The Lord is your shepherd. Trust Him today and be blessed.

11

THE PROMISE: IF YOU HAVE FAITH, YOU CAN MOVE MOUNTAINS

For truly I say to you, if you have faith the size of a mustard seed, you will say to this mountain, "Move from here to there," and it will move; and nothing will be impossible to you.

MATTHEW 17:20 NASB

Because we live in a demanding world, all of us have mountains to climb and mountains to move. Moving those mountains requires faith. Are you a mountain-moving person whose faith is evident for all to see? Or are you more fearful than that? As you think about the answer to that question, consider this: God needs more people who are willing to try new things, to take big steps, and to move mountains for the glory of His kingdom.

Is your faith strong enough to move the mountains in your own life? If so, you've already tapped in to a source of strength that never fails: God's strength. But if your spiritual batteries are in need of recharging, don't be discouraged. God's strength is always available to those who seek it.

The first element of a successful life is faith: faith in God, faith in His promises, and faith in His Son. When our faith in the Creator is strong, we can then have faith in ourselves, knowing that we are tools in the hands of a loving God who made mountains—and moves them—according to a perfect plan that only He can see.

MORE THOUGHTS ABOUT FAITH

Faith is confidence in
the promises of God
or confidence that God will
do what He has promised.

CHARLES STANLEY

I do not want merely to possess a faith; I
want a faith that possesses me.

CHARLES KINGSLEY

Shout the shout of faith.
Nothing can withstand the
triumphant faith that links itself
to omnipotence. The secret
of all successful living lies
in this shout of faith.

HANNAH WHITALL SMITH

How do you walk in faith? By claiming the promises
of God and obeying the Word of God, in spite of
what you see, how you feel, or what may happen.

WARREN WIERSBE

MORE FROM GOD'S WORD

Don't be afraid, because I am your God. I will make you strong and will help you; I will support you with my right hand that saves you.

ISAIAH 41:10 NCV

Don't be afraid. Only believe.

MARK 5:36 HCSB

Blessed are they that have not seen, and yet have believed.

JOHN 20:29 KJV

All things are possible for the one who believes.

MARK 9:23 NCV

And he said unto her, Daughter, thy faith hath made thee whole; go in peace, and be whole.

MARK 5:34 KJV

REMEMBER THIS

Faith should be practiced more than studied. Vance Havner said, "Nothing is more disastrous than to study faith, analyze faith, make noble resolves of faith, but never actually to make the leap of faith." How true.

12

THE PROMISE: GOD'S TIMING IS PERFECT

*He has made everything appropriate in its time. He has
also put eternity in their hearts, but man cannot discover
the work God has done from beginning to end.*

ECCLESIASTES 3:11 HCSB

If you're enduring difficult times—or if your thoughts have been hijacked by feelings of anxiety or doubt—you're understandably in a hurry for things to improve. You want solutions to your problems as quickly as possible, preferably today. And because your time on earth is limited, you may feel a sense of urgency. You want a quick resolution, and you want to move on with your life. But God may have other plans.

Our heavenly Father, in His infinite wisdom, operates according to His own timetable, not ours. He has plans that we cannot see and purposes that we cannot know. He has created a world that unfolds according to His own schedule. Thank goodness! After all, He is omniscient; His is trustworthy; and He knows what's best for us.

If you've been waiting impatiently for the Lord to answer your prayers, it's time to put a stop to all that needless worry. You can be sure that God will answer your prayers when the time is right. You job is to keep praying—and working—until He does.

MORE THOUGHTS ABOUT GOD'S TIMING

We must learn to move according to the timetable
of the Timeless One, and to be at peace.

ELISABETH ELLIOT

The Christian's journey through life
isn't a sprint but a marathon.

BILLY GRAHAM

Teach us, O Lord, the disciplines of patience,
for to wait is often harder than to work.

PETER MARSHALL

Waiting is the hardest kind of work, but God knows
best, and we may joyfully leave all in His hands.

LOTTIE MOON

We often hear about waiting on God, which actually means that
He is waiting until we are ready. There is another side, however.
When we wait for God, we are waiting until He is ready.

LETTIE COWMAN

MORE FROM GOD'S WORD

Therefore humble yourselves under the mighty hand of God, that He may exalt you in due time.

1 Peter 5:6 NKJV

Those who trust in the LORD are like Mount Zion. It cannot be shaken; it remains forever.

Psalm 125:1 HCSB

Yet the LORD longs to be gracious to you; therefore he will rise up to show you compassion. For the LORD is a God of justice. Blessed are all who wait for him!

Isaiah 30:18 NIV

Trust in the LORD with all your heart, and lean not on your own understanding; in all your ways acknowledge Him, and He shall direct your paths.

Proverbs 3:5–6 NKJV

To every thing there is a season, and a time to every purpose under the heaven.

Ecclesiastes 3:1 KJV

REMEMBER THIS

God is never early or late. He's always on time. Although you don't know precisely what you need—or when you need it—He does. So trust His timing.

13

THE PROMISE OF SPIRITUAL GROWTH

I remind you to fan into flames the spiritual gift God gave you.

2 TIMOTHY 1:6 NLT

When it comes to your faith, God doesn't intend for you to stand still. He wants you to keep moving and growing. In fact, God's plan for you includes a lifetime of prayer, praise, and spiritual growth.

When we cease to grow, either emotionally or spiritually, we do ourselves and our loved ones a profound disservice. But if we study God's Word, if we obey His commandments, and if we live in the center of His will, our faith will grow.

Many of life's most important lessons are painful to learn. During times of uncertainty or hardship, we must be courageous and we must be patient, knowing that in His own time, God will heal us if we invite Him into our hearts.

Spiritual growth need not take place only in times of adversity. We can grow in our knowledge and love of the Lord through every season of life. In those quiet moments when we open our hearts to Him, the One who made us keeps remaking us. He gives us direction, perspective, wisdom, and courage. The appropriate moment to accept those spiritual gifts is the present one.

Are you as mature as you're ever going to be? Hopefully not. When it comes to your faith, God doesn't intend for you to become "fully grown," at least not in this lifetime. In fact, the Lord still has important lessons that He intends to teach you. So ask yourself this:

What lesson is God trying to teach me today? And then go about the business of learning it.

MORE THOUGHTS ABOUT SPIRITUAL GROWTH

Daily Bible reading is essential to victorious
living and real Christian growth.

BILLY GRAHAM

The Scriptures were not given for our
information, but for our transformation.

D. L. MOODY

The vigor of our spiritual lives
will be in exact proportion to the place held by
the Bible in our lives and in our thoughts.

GEORGE MUELLER

Grow, dear friends, but grow,
I beseech you, in God's way,
which is the only true way.

HANNAH WHITALL SMITH

Kindness in this world will do much
to help others, not only to come into the light,
but also to grow in grace day by day.

FANNY CROSBY

MORE FROM GOD'S WORD

But endurance must do its complete work, so that you may be mature and complete, lacking nothing.

JAMES 1:4 HCSB

But grow in the grace and knowledge of our Lord and Savior Jesus Christ. To Him be the glory both now and forever. Amen.

2 PETER 3:18 NKJV

And be not conformed to this world: but be ye transformed by the renewing of your mind, that ye may prove what is that good, and acceptable, and perfect, will of God.

ROMANS 12:2 KJV

Leave inexperience behind, and you will live; pursue the way of understanding.

PROVERBS 9:6 HCSB

So let us stop going over the basic teachings about Christ again and again. Let us go on instead and become mature in our understanding.

HEBREWS 6:1 NLT

A TIMELY TIP

Uncertain times have many lessons to teach—lessons that we desperately need to learn. And we should always remember that spiritual maturity is a journey, not a destination.

14

THE PROMISE: DURING UNCERTAIN TIMES, THE LORD IS YOUR REFUGE

God is our protection and our strength. He
always helps in times of trouble.

PSALM 46:1 NCV

All of us must endure difficult circumstances, those times of uncertainty when our faith is tested and our strength is stretched to the limit. We find ourselves in situations that we didn't ask for and probably don't deserve. During those difficult days, we try our best to "hold up under the circumstances." But God has a better plan. He intends for us to rise above our circumstances, and He's promised to help us do it.

Are you dealing with a difficult situation or a tough problem? Do you struggle with occasional periods of anxiety or doubt? Are you worried, weary, or downcast? If so, don't face tough times alone. Face them with God as your partner, your protector, and your guide. Talk to Him often, ask for His guidance, and listen carefully for His response. When you do, He will give you the strength meet any challenge, the courage to face any problem, and the patience to endure—and to eventually rise above—any circumstance.

DEALING WITH DIFFICULT CIRCUMSTANCES

No matter what our circumstance, we
can find a reason to be thankful.

DAVID JEREMIAH

God has a purpose behind every problem. He uses
circumstances to develop our character. In fact,
he depends more on circumstances to make us like
Jesus than he depends on our reading the Bible.

RICK WARREN

Every experience God gives us, every person he
brings into our lives, is the perfect preparation
for the future that only he can see.

CORRIE TEN BOOM

Oftentimes God demonstrates His faithfulness in adversity by
providing for us what we need to survive. He does not change
our painful circumstances. He sustains us through them.

CHARLES STANLEY

Don't let obstacles along the road to eternity
shake your confidence in God's promises.

DAVID JEREMIAH

MORE FROM GOD'S WORD

I have learned in whatever state I am, to be content.

PHILIPPIANS 4:11 NKJV

*Trust in him at all times, you people; pour out
your hearts to him, for God is our refuge.*

PSALM 62:8 NIV

The LORD is a refuge for His people and a stronghold.

JOEL 3:16 NASB

The LORD is a refuge for the oppressed, a refuge in times of trouble.

PSALM 9:9 HCSB

*Cast your burden on the LORD, and He shall sustain you;
He shall never permit the righteous to be moved.*

PSALM 55:22 NKJV

REMEMBER THIS

A change of circumstances is rarely as important as a change in attitude. If you change your thoughts, you will most certainly change your circumstances.

15

THE PROMISE OF PERSPECTIVE: WHEN YOU TRUST GOD'S PROMISES AND KEEP TODAY'S CHALLENGES IN PROPER PERSPECTIVE, YOU'LL BE AT PEACE

Joyful is the person who finds wisdom,
the one who gains understanding.

PROVERBS 3:13 NLT

For most of us, life is busy and complicated. Amid the rush and crush of the daily grind, it is easy to lose perspective . . . easy, but wrong. When the world seems to be spinning out of control, we can regain perspective by slowing ourselves down and then turning our thoughts and prayers toward God.

The familiar words of Psalm 46:10 remind us to "Be still, and know that I am God" (NKJV). When we do so, we are reminded of God's love (not to mention God's priorities), and we can then refocus our thoughts on the things that matter most. But when we ignore the presence of our Creator—if we rush from place to place with scarcely a spare minute for God—we rob ourselves of His perspective, His peace, and His joy.

Do you carve out quiet moments each day to offer thanksgiving and praise to your Creator? You should. During these moments, you will often sense the love and wisdom of our Lord. So today and every day, make time to be still before God. When you do, you can face the day's complications with the wisdom, the perspective, and the power that only He can provide.

MORE THOUGHTS ABOUT PERSPECTIVE

What you see and hear depends a good deal on where you are standing; it also depends on what sort of person you are.

C. S. LEWIS

When you and I hurt deeply, what we really need is not an explanation from God but a revelation of God. We need to see how great God is; we need to recover our lost perspective on life. Things get out of proportion when we are suffering, and it takes a vision of something bigger than ourselves to get life's dimensions adjusted again.

WARREN WIERSBE

Joy is the direct result of having God's perspective on our daily lives and the effect of loving our Lord enough to obey His commands and trust His promises.

BILL BRIGHT

Perspective is everything when you are experiencing the challenges of life.

JONI EARECKSON TADA

Earthly fears are no fears at all.
Answer the big question of eternity, and the little questions of life fall into perspective.

MAX LUCADO

MORE FROM GOD'S WORD

If you teach the wise, they will get knowledge.

PROVERBS 21:11 NCV

*The one who acquires good sense loves himself; one
who safeguards understanding finds success.*

PROVERBS 19:8 HCSB

*Since you have been raised to new life with Christ, set
your sights on the realities of heaven, where Christ
sits in the place of honor at God's right hand.*

COLOSSIANS 3:1 NLT

*Teach me, LORD, the meaning of Your statutes,
and I will always keep them.*

PSALM 119:33 HCSB

*Trust in the LORD with all your heart and lean
not on your own understanding.*

PROVERBS 3:5 NIV

A TIMELY TIP

Remember that your life is an integral part of God's grand plan.
So don't become unduly upset over the minor inconveniences of
everyday life, and don't worry too much about today's setbacks—
they're temporary.

16

THE PROMISE: THE LORD CAN GIVE YOU THE COURAGE AND THE STRENGTH TO MEET ANY CHALLENGE

Be strong and courageous, and do the work. Do not be afraid or discouraged, for the LORD God, my God, is with you.

1 CHRONICLES 28:20 NIV

As believers in a risen Christ, we can, and should, live courageously. After all, Jesus promises that He has overcome the world and that He has made a place for us in heaven. So we have nothing to fear in the long term because our Lord will care for us throughout eternity. But what about those short-term, everyday worries that keep us up at night? And what about the life-altering hardships that leave us wondering if we can ever recover? The answer, of course, is that because God cares for us in good times and uncertain times, we can turn our concerns over to Him in prayer, knowing that all things ultimately work for the good of those who love Him.

At this very moment the Lord is seeking to work in you and through you. He's asking you to live abundantly and courageously, and He's ready to help. So why not let Him do it, starting now?

MORE THOUGHTS ABOUT COURAGE

Take courage. We walk in the wilderness today
and in the Promised Land tomorrow.

D. L. MOODY

Courage is not simply one of the virtues, but the
form of every virtue at the testing point.

C. S. LEWIS

Just as courage is faith in good, so discouragement
is faith in evil, and, while courage opens the door
to good, discouragement opens it to evil.

HANNAH WHITALL SMITH

In my experience, God rarely makes our fear disappear.
Instead, he asks us to be strong and take courage.

BRUCE WILKINSON

Do not let Satan deceive you into being
afraid of God's plans for your life.

R. A. TORREY

MORE FROM GOD'S WORD

Be on guard. Stand firm in the faith.
Be courageous. Be strong.

1 CORINTHIANS 16:13 NLT

For God has not given us a spirit of fearfulness, but
one of power, love, and sound judgment.

2 TIMOTHY 1:7 HCSB

I can do all things through Him who strengthens me.

PHILIPPIANS 4:13 NASB

But He said to them, "It is I; do not be afraid."

JOHN 6:20 NKJV

Behold, God is my salvation; I will trust, and not be afraid.

ISAIAH 12:2 KJV

A TIMELY TIP

Is your courage being tested today? Cling tightly to God's promises, and pray. The Lord can give you the strength to meet any challenge, and that's exactly what you should ask Him to do.

17

THE PROMISE: WHEN YOU TRUST GOD COMPLETELY, YOUR FUTURE IS BRIGHT

There is surely a future hope for you,
and your hope will not be cut off.

PROVERBS 23:18 NIV

If you've entrusted your heart to Christ, your eternal fate is secure and your future is eternally bright. No matter how troublesome your present circumstances may seem, you need not fear because the Lord has promised that you are His now and forever.

Of course, you won't be exempt from the normal challenges of life here on earth. While you're here, you'll probably experience your fair share of disappointments, defeats, emergencies, and outright failures. But these are only temporary setbacks.

Are you willing to place your future in the hands of a loving and all-knowing God? Do you trust in the ultimate goodness of His plan for you? Will you face today's challenges with hope and optimism? You should. After all, the Lord created you for a very important purpose: His purpose. And you still have important work to do: His work. So today as you live in the present and look to the future, remember that God has a marvelous plan for you. Act—and believe—accordingly.

MORE THOUGHTS ABOUT THE FUTURE

Never be afraid to trust an
unknown future to a known God.

CORRIE TEN BOOM

Our future may look fearfully
intimidating, yet we can look up to
the Engineer of the Universe,
confident that nothing escapes His
attention or slips out of the
control of those strong hands.

ELISABETH ELLIOT

Knowing that your future is absolutely assured
can free you to live abundantly today.

SARAH YOUNG

It may be that the day of judgment will dawn
tomorrow; in that case, we shall gladly stop
working for a better future. But not before.

DIETRICH BONHOEFFER

Every experience God gives us, every person he
brings into our lives, is the perfect preparation
for the future that only he can see.

CORRIE TEN BOOM

MORE FROM GOD'S WORD

For I know the thoughts that I think toward you, says the LORD, thoughts of peace and not of evil, to give you a future and a hope. Then you will call upon Me and go and pray to Me, and I will listen to you.

JEREMIAH 29:11–12 NKJV

The LORD is my light and my salvation—whom should I fear? The LORD is the stronghold of my life—of whom should I be afraid?

PSALM 27:1 HCSB

But if we look forward to something we don't yet have, we must wait patiently and confidently.

ROMANS 8:25 NLT

Wisdom is pleasing to you. If you find it, you have hope for the future.

PROVERBS 24:14 NCV

Rest in God alone, my soul, for my hope comes from Him.

PSALM 62:5 HCSB

A TIMELY TIP

Your future here on earth depends, to a very great extent, upon you. So keep learning and keep growing personally, intellectually, emotionally, and spiritually.

18

THE PROMISE: THE LORD WILL GUIDE YOU THROUGH UNCERTAIN TIMES IF YOU LET HIM

*The LORD says, "I will guide you along the best pathway
for your life. I will advise you and watch over you."*

PSALM 32:8 NLT

When we ask for God's guidance with our hearts and minds open to His direction, He will lead us along a path of His choosing. But for many of us, listening to God is hard. We have so many things we want—and so many needs to pray for—that we spend far more time talking at God than we do listening to Him.

Corrie ten Boom observed, "God's guidance is even more important than common sense. I can declare that the deepest darkness is outshone by the light of Jesus." These words remind us that life is best lived when we seek the Lord's direction early and often.

Our Father has many ways to make Himself known. Our challenge is to make ourselves open to His instruction. So if you're unsure of your next step, trust God's promises and talk to Him often. When you do, He'll guide your steps today, tomorrow, and forever.

MORE THOUGHTS ABOUT GOD'S GUIDANCE

God never leads us to do anything
that is contrary to the Bible.

BILLY GRAHAM

When we are obedient,
God guides our steps and our stops.

CORRIE TEN BOOM

Are you serious about wanting God's guidance
to become a personal reality in your life? The
first step is to tell God that you know you can't
manage your own life; that you need his help.

CATHERINE MARSHALL

The will of God will never take us where the
grace of God cannot sustain us.

BILLY GRAHAM

As you walk through the valley of the unknown, you will find
the footprints of Jesus both in front of you and beside you.

CHARLES STANLEY

MORE FROM GOD'S WORD

Yet Lord, You are our Father; we are the clay, and You are our potter; we all are the work of Your hands.

Isaiah 64:8 HCSB

Trust in the Lord with all your heart, and lean not on your own understanding; in all your ways acknowledge Him, and He shall direct your paths.

Proverbs 3:5–6 NKJV

Teach me to do Your will, for You are my God; Your Spirit is good. Lead me in the land of uprightness.

Psalm 143:10 NKJV

Shew me thy ways, O Lord; teach me thy paths. Lead me in thy truth, and teach me: for thou art the God of my salvation; on thee do I wait all the day.

Psalm 25:4–5 KJV

Morning by morning he wakens me and opens my understanding to his will. The Sovereign Lord has spoken to me, and I have listened.

Isaiah 50:4–5 NLT

A TIMELY TIP

Would you like God's guidance? Then ask Him for it. When you pray for guidance, God will give it. So ask.

19

THE PROMISE: NO PROBLEMS ARE TOO BIG FOR GOD

People who do what is right may have many problems, but the LORD will solve them all.

PSALM 34:19 NCV

Life is an adventure in problem-solving. The question is not whether we will encounter problems; the real question is how we will choose to address them. When it comes to solving the problems of everyday living, we often know precisely what needs to be done, but we may be slow in doing it, especially if what needs to be done is difficult. So we put off until tomorrow what should be done today.

As a person living here in the twenty-first century, you have your own set of challenges. As you face those challenges, you may be comforted by this fact: trouble, of every kind, is temporary. Yet God's grace is eternal. And worries, of every kind, are temporary. But God's love is everlasting. The difficulties that concern you will pass. God remains. And for every problem, God has a solution.

The words of Psalm 34 remind us that the Lord solves problems for "people who do what is right." And usually, doing "what is right" means doing the uncomfortable work of confronting our problems sooner rather than later. So with no further ado, let the problem-solving begin . . . right now.

MORE THOUGHTS ABOUT PROBLEM-SOLVING

We are all faced with a series of great opportunities,
brilliantly disguised as unsolvable problems.
Unsolvable without God's wisdom, that is.

CHARLES SWINDOLL

Life will be made or broken at the place where
we meet and deal with obstacles.

E. STANLEY JONES

Each problem is a God-appointed instructor.

CHARLES SWINDOLL

God is bigger than your problems.
Whatever worries press upon you today, put
them in God's hands and leave them there.

BILLY GRAHAM

MORE FROM GOD'S WORD

*We are pressured in every way but not crushed;
we are perplexed but not in despair.*

2 CORINTHIANS 4:8 HCSB

Consider it a great joy, my brothers,
whenever you experience various trials,
knowing that the testing of your faith produces
endurance. But endurance must do its
complete work, so that you may be mature
and complete, lacking nothing.

JAMES 1:2 HCSB

We also have joy with our troubles, because we know
that these troubles produce patience. And patience
produces character, and character produces hope.

ROMANS 5:3–4 NCV

Trust the LORD your God with all your heart and lean
not on your own understanding; in all your ways submit
to him, and he will make your paths straight.

PROVERBS 3:5–6 NIV

I have learned in whatever state I am, to be content.

PHILIPPIANS 4:11 NKJV

A TIMELY TIP

Today, think about the wisdom of tackling your problems sooner rather than later. Remember that "this, too, will pass," but whatever "it" is will pass more quickly if you spend more time solving your problems and less time fretting about them.

20

THE PROMISE: BECAUSE THE LORD IS FAITHFUL, YOU CAN THINK OPTIMISTICALLY

The LORD is my light and my salvation—whom should I fear? The LORD is the stronghold of my life—of whom should I be afraid?

PSALM 27:1 HCSB

As a believer in Christ, you have every reason to be confident about your future here on earth and your eternal future in heaven. As English clergyman William Ralph Inge observed, "No Christian should be a pessimist, for Christianity is a system of radical optimism." Inge's observation is true, of course, but sometimes you may find yourself caught up in the stress-inducing distractions of an anxious age. When you find yourself fretting about the inevitable ups, downs, and of twenty-first-century life, it's time to slow down, collect yourself, refocus your thoughts, and count your blessings.

The Lord has made many promises to you, and He will most certainly keep every single one of them. So you have every reason to be an optimist and no legitimate reason to abandon hope. So today trust your hopes, not your fears. And while you're at it, take time to celebrate God's blessings. His gifts are too numerous to calculate and too glorious to imagine. But, it never hurts to try.

MORE THOUGHTS ABOUT OPTIMISM

Two types of voices command your attention
today. Negative ones fill your mind with doubt,
bitterness, and fear. Positive ones purvey hope and
strength. Which one will you choose to heed?

MAX LUCADO

Have a sincere desire to serve God and mankind, and
stop doubting. Stop thinking negatively. Simply start
living by faith, pray earnestly and humbly, and get
into the habit of looking expectantly for the best.

NORMAN VINCENT PEALE

All things work together for good. Fret not, nor fear!

LETTIE COWMAN

Take courage. We walk in the wilderness today
and in the Promised Land tomorrow.

D. L. MOODY

Faith is deliberate confidence in the character of God
whose ways you may not understand at the time.

OSWALD CHAMBERS

MORE FROM GOD'S WORD

Make me to hear joy and gladness.

PSALM 51:8 KJV

But if we look forward to something we don't yet have, we must wait patiently and confidently.

ROMANS 8:25 NLT

"I say this because I know what I am planning for you," says the LORD. "I have good plans for you, not plans to hurt you. I will give you hope and a good future."

JEREMIAH 29:11 NCV

This hope we have as an anchor of the soul, a hope both sure and steadfast.

HEBREWS 6:19 NASB

Let us hold on to the confession of our hope without wavering, for He who promised is faithful.

HEBREWS 10:23 HCSB

A TIMELY TIP

Be a realistic optimist. Your attitude toward the future will help create your future. So think realistically about yourself and your situation while making a conscious effort to focus on hopes, not fears. When you do, you'll put the self-fulfilling prophecy to work for you.

21

THE PROMISE: YOUR GOOD WORKS WILL BEAR FRUIT

But this I say: He who sows sparingly will also reap sparingly,
and he who sows bountifully will also reap bountifully.

2 CORINTHIANS 9:6 NKJV

The old saying is both familiar and true: We should pray as if everything depended upon the Lord but work as if everything depended upon us. Yet sometimes, when we are tired or discouraged, our worries can sap our strength and sidetrack our motivation. But God has other intentions. He expects us to work for the things that we pray for. More importantly, He intends that our work should become His work.

The book of Proverbs teaches us that, "One who is slack in his work is brother to one who destroys" (18:9 NIV). Clearly, God's Word commends the value and importance of diligence, yet we live in a world that, all too often, glorifies leisure while downplaying the importance of shoulder-to-the wheel hard work. Rest assured, however, that the Lord does not underestimate the value of diligence. And neither should you.

As you seek to accomplish your goals and fulfill God's plan for your life, remember that your success will depend, in large part, upon the passion that you bring to your work. The Lord has created a world in which hard work is rewarded and laziness is not. So don't look for shortcuts (because there aren't any) and don't expect easy solutions to life's biggest challenges (because big rewards usually require lots of effort). You inhabit a world in which instant gratification is rare, but the rewards of hard work are not. Shape your expectations—and your work habits—accordingly.

MORE THOUGHTS ABOUT WORK

God did not intend for us to be idle and
unproductive. There is dignity in work.

BILLY GRAHAM

Ordinary work, which is what most of us do most of the time,
is ordained by God every bit as much as is the extraordinary.

ELISABETH ELLIOT

It may be that the day of judgment will dawn
tomorrow; in that case, we shall gladly stop
working for a better future. But not before.

DIETRICH BONHOEFFER

When love and skill work together,
expect a masterpiece.

JOHN RUSKIN

The things, good Lord, that I pray for,
give me the grace to labor for.

THOMAS MORE

MORE FROM GOD'S WORD

*Whatever you do, do it enthusiastically, as
something done for the Lord and not for men.*

COLOSSIANS 3:23 HCSB

*Be strong and courageous, and do the work. Don't be
afraid or discouraged, for the LORD God, my God, is
with you. He won't leave you or forsake you.*

1 CHRONICLES 28:20 HCSB

*The plans of hard-working people earn a profit, but
those who act too quickly become poor.*

PROVERBS 21:5 NCV

*Do you see a man skilled in his work? He
will stand in the presence of kings.*

PROVERBS 22:29 HCSB

*I must work the works of Him who sent Me while it is
day; the night is coming when no one can work.*

JOHN 9:4 NKJV

A TIMELY TIP

Here's a time-tested formula for success: have faith in God and
do the work. So remember that hard work is not simply a proven
way to get ahead; it's also part of God's plan for all His children
(including you).

22

THE PROMISE: WHEN YOU BECOME A COMPLAINT-FREE ZONE, YOU WILL BE BLESSED

My dear brothers and sisters, always be
willing to listen and slow to speak.

JAMES 1:19 NCV

Most of us have more blessings than we can count, yet we still find things to complain about. To complain, of course, is not only short-sighted, but it is also a serious roadblock on the path to spiritual abundance. Yet in our weakest moments we still grumble, whine, and moan about difficult people or the difficult circumstances they seem to create. Sometimes we give voice to our complaints, and on other occasions, we manage to keep our protestations to ourselves. But even when no one else hears our complaints, God does.

Would you like to feel more comfortable about your circumstances and your life? Then promise yourself that you'll do whatever it takes to focus your thoughts on the major blessings you've received, not the minor hardships—or the difficult circumstances—you must occasionally endure.

So the next time you're tempted to complain about the inevitable frustrations of everyday life, don't do it. Today and every day, make it a practice to count your blessings, not your inconveniences. It's the truly decent way to live.

MAKE YOUR MIND A COMPLAINT-FREE ZONE

Thanksgiving or complaining—these words express two
contrasting attitudes of the souls of God's children. The
soul that gives thanks can find comfort in everything;
the soul that complains can find comfort in nothing.

HANNAH WHITALL SMITH

It is always possible to be thankful for what is given
rather than to complain about what is not given.
One or the other becomes a habit of life.

ELISABETH ELLIOT

Don't complain. The more you complain about things,
the more things you'll have to complain about.

E. STANLEY JONES

Grumbling and gratitude are, for the child of God,
in conflict. Be grateful and you won't grumble.
Grumble and you won't be grateful.

BILLY GRAHAM

Trust and thankfulness will get you safely through this
day. Trust protects you from worrying and obsessing.
Thankfulness keeps you from criticizing and complaining.

SARAH YOUNG

MORE FROM GOD'S WORD

Be hospitable to one another without complaining.

1 Peter 4:9 HCSB

Do everything without complaining or arguing. Then you will be innocent and without any wrong.

Philippians 2:14–15 NCV

Those who guard their lips preserve their lives, but those who speak rashly will come to ruin.

Proverbs 13:3 NIV

A fool's displeasure is known at once, but whoever ignores an insult is sensible.

Proverbs 12:16 HCSB

Those who consider themselves religious and yet do not keep a tight rein on their tongues deceive themselves, and their religion is worthless.

James 1:26 NIV

A TIMELY TIP

If you feel a personal pity party coming on, slow down and start counting your blessings. If you fill your heart with gratitude, there's simply no room left for complaints.

23

THE PROMISE: FAILURE ISN'T FINAL

One who listens to life-giving rebukes
will be at home among the wise.

PROVERBS 15:31 HCSB

Life's occasional setbacks are simply the price that we must pay for our willingness to take risks as we follow our dreams. But even when we encounter bitter disappointments, we must never lose faith.

Hebrews 10:36 advises, "Patient endurance is what you need now, so that you will continue to do God's will. Then you will receive all that he has promised" (NLT). These words remind us that when we persevere, we will eventually receive the rewards which God has promised us. What's required is perseverance, not perfection.

When we face hardships or failures, the Lord stands ready to protect us. Our responsibility, of course, is to ask Him for protection. When we call upon Him in heartfelt prayer, He will answer—in His own time and according to His own plan—and He will do His part to heal us. We, of course, must do our part too. And while we are waiting for God's plans to unfold and for His healing touch to restore us, we can be comforted in the knowledge that our Creator can overcome any obstacle, even if we cannot.

MORE THOUGHTS ABOUT FAILURE

The enemy of our souls loves to taunt us
with past failures, wrongs, disappointments,
disasters, and calamities. And if we let him
continue doing this, our life becomes a long and
dark tunnel, with very little light at the end.

CHARLES SWINDOLL

What may seem defeat to
us may be victory to him.

C. H. SPURGEON

Success or failure can be pretty
well predicted by the degree to
which the heart is fully in it.

JOHN ELDREDGE

Never imagine that you can
be a loser by trusting in God.

C. H. SPURGEON

Goals are worth setting and worth missing.
We learn from non-successes.

BILL BRIGHT

MORE FROM GOD'S WORD

Though the righteous fall seven times, they rise again.

PROVERBS 24:16 NIV

The LORD is near to those who have a broken heart.

PSALM 34:18 NKJV

*If you listen to correction to improve your
life, you will live among the wise.*

PROVERBS 15:31 NCV

*We are hard-pressed on every side, yet not crushed;
we are perplexed, but not in despair.*

2 CORINTHIANS 4:8 NKJV

*But as for you, be strong; don't be discouraged,
for your work has a reward.*

2 CHRONICLES 15:7 HCSB

REMEMBER THIS

Failure isn't permanent *unless* you fail to get up. So the next time you experience a setback, pick yourself up, dust yourself off, and trust God. He will make it right. Warren Wiersbe had this advice: "No matter how badly we have failed, we can always get up and begin again. Our God is the God of new beginnings." And don't forget: the best time to begin again is now.

24

THE PROMISE OF RENEWAL

You are being renewed in the spirit of your minds; you put on the new self, the one created according to God's likeness in righteousness and purity of the truth.

EPHESIANS 4:23–24 HCSB

For busy citizens of the twenty-first century, it's easy to become overcommitted, overworked, and overstressed. If we choose, we can be connected 24-7, sparing just enough time to a few hours' sleep each night. What we need is time to renew and recharge, but finding the time seems difficult. So instead of slowing down and talking to our Creator, we speed up and suffer the consequences.

God can renew your strength and restore your spirits if you let Him. But He won't force you to slow down, and He won't insist that you get enough sleep at night. He leaves those choices up to you.

If you're feeling chronically tired or discouraged, it's time to rearrange your schedule, turn off every screen, and spend quiet time with your heavenly Father. He knows what you need, and He wants you to experience His peace and His love. He's ready, willing, and perfectly able to renew your strength and help you prioritize the items on your do-list if you ask Him. In fact, He's ready to hear your prayers right now. Please don't make Him wait.

MORE THOUGHTS ABOUT RENEWAL

Troubles we bear trustfully can bring us a fresh vision of God
and a new outlook on life, an outlook of peace and hope.

BILLY GRAHAM

Walking with God leads to receiving his intimate
counsel, and counseling leads to deep restoration.

JOHN ELDREDGE

The same voice that brought Lazarus out of
the tomb raised us to newness of life.

C. H. SPURGEON

When we reach the end of our strength,
wisdom, and personal resources, we enter into
the beginning of his glorious provisions.

PATSY CLAIRMONT

He is the God of wholeness and restoration.

STORMIE OMARTIAN

MORE FROM GOD'S WORD

*Therefore, if anyone is in Christ, he is a new creation; old things
have passed away; behold, all things have become new.*

2 CORINTHIANS 5:17 NKJV

*So we're not giving up. How could we! Even though on
the outside it often looks like things are falling apart
on us, on the inside, where God is making new life,
not a day goes by without his unfolding grace.*

2 CORINTHIANS 4:16 MSG

*No matter how many times you trip them up, God-loyal
people don't stay down long; soon they're up on their
feet, while the wicked end up flat on their faces.*

PROVERBS 24:16 MSG

For I am Yahweh who heals you.

EXODUS 15:26 HCSB

REMEMBER THIS

God can make all things new, including you. When you are weak or
worried, He can renew your spirit and restore your strength. Your
job, of course, is to let Him.

25

THE PROMISE: WHEN YOU GUARD YOUR HEART AND YOUR THOUGHTS, YOU WILL BE BLESSED

Finally, brothers and sisters, whatever is true,
whatever is noble, whatever is right, whatever is pure,
whatever is lovely, whatever is admirable—if anything
is excellent or praiseworthy—think about such things.

PHILIPPIANS 4:8 NIV

Your thoughts are intensely powerful things. Thoughts have the power to lift you up or drag you down; they have the power to energize you or deplete you, to inspire you to greater accomplishments or to make those accomplishments impossible.

How will you direct your thoughts today? Will you obey the words of Philippians 4:8 by dwelling upon those things that are noble and admirable? Or will you allow your thoughts to be hijacked by the negativity that seems to dominate our troubled world?

It's up to you to celebrate the life that God has given you by focusing your minds upon things that are excellent and praiseworthy. So form the habit of spending more time thinking about your blessings and less time fretting about your hardships. Then take time to thank your heavenly Father for gifts that are, in truth, far too numerous to count.

MORE THOUGHTS ABOUT GUARDING YOUR THOUGHTS

The mind is like a clock that is constantly
running down. It has to be wound
up daily with good thoughts.

FULTON J. SHEEN

It is the thoughts and intents of the
heart that shape a person's life.

JOHN ELDREDGE

The things we think are the things
that feed our souls. If we think on pure
and lovely things, we shall grow pure and lovely
like them; and the converse is equally true.

HANNAH WHITALL SMITH

When you think on the powerful
truths of Scripture, God uses His Word
to change your way of thinking.

ELIZABETH GEORGE

Your life today is a result of your
thinking yesterday. Your life tomorrow will
be determined by what you think today.

JOHN MAXWELL

MORE FROM GOD'S WORD

Guard your heart above all else, for it is the source of life.

PROVERBS 4:23 HCSB

Set your mind on things above, not on things on the earth.

COLOSSIANS 3:2 NKJV

The peace of God, which surpasses all understanding, will guard your hearts and minds through Christ Jesus.

PHILIPPIANS 4:7 NKJV

And do not be conformed to this world, but be transformed by the renewing of your mind, so that you may prove what the will of God is, that which is good and acceptable and perfect.

ROMANS 12:2 NASB

For to be carnally minded is death, but to be spiritually minded is life and peace.

ROMANS 8:6 NKJV

A TIMELY TIP

Watch what you think. If your inner voice is, in reality, your inner critic, you need to tone down the criticism now. And while you're at it, train yourself to begin thinking thoughts that are more rational, more accepting, and less judgmental.

26

THE PROMISE: PERSEVERANCE PAYS

For you have need of endurance, so that when you have done
the will of God, you may receive what was promised.

HEBREWS 10:36 NASB

Occasionally, good things happen with little or no effort. Somebody inherits a fortune or wins the lottery or stumbles onto a financial bonanza by being at the right place at the right time. But more often than not, good things happen to people who work hard and keep working hard.

Calvin Coolidge observed that, "Nothing in the world can take the place of persistence. Talent will not; genius will not; education will not. Persistence and determination alone are omnipotent." President Coolidge was right. Perseverance pays.

Perhaps you are in a hurry for God to help you resolve your difficulties. Perhaps you're anxious to reap the rewards that you feel you've already earned from life. Perhaps you're drumming your fingers, impatiently waiting for God to act. If so, be forewarned: the Lord operates on His own timetable, not yours. Sometimes, He may answer your prayers with silence, and when He does, you must patiently persevere.

So when it comes to your physical, emotional, or spiritual fitness, don't give up and don't give in. Just keep putting one foot in front of the other, pray for strength, live in day-tight compartments, and keep going. Whether you realize it or not, you're up to the challenge if you persevere. And with God's help, that's exactly what you'll do.

MORE THOUGHTS ABOUT PERSEVERANCE

Jesus taught that perseverance is the
essential element in prayer.

E. M. BOUNDS

Perseverance is more than endurance. It is endurance
combined with absolute assurance and certainty
that what we are looking for is going to happen.

OSWALD CHAMBERS

Battles are won in the trenches, in the grit
and grime of courageous determination; they
are won day by day in the arena of life.

CHARLES SWINDOLL

Let us not cease to do the utmost, that we may
incessantly go forward in the way of the Lord; and let us
not despair of the smallness of our accomplishments.

JOHN CALVIN

Don't quit. For if you do, you may miss
the answer to your prayers.

MAX LUCADO

MORE FROM GOD'S WORD

Let us not become weary in doing good, for at the proper
time we will reap a harvest if we do not give up.

GALATIANS 6:9 NIV

But as for you, be strong; don't be discouraged,
for your work has a reward.

2 CHRONICLES 15:7 HCSB

We are hard-pressed on every side, yet not crushed;
we are perplexed, but not in despair.

2 CORINTHIANS 4:8 NKJV

Finishing is better than starting. Patience is better than pride.

ECCLESIASTES 7:8 NLT

So let us run the race that is before us and never give up.
We should remove from our lives anything that would get
in the way and the sin that so easily holds us back.

HEBREWS 12:1 NCV

A TIMELY TIP

Whenever you are being tested, you can call upon God, and you
should. The Lord can give you the strength to persevere, and that's
exactly what you should ask Him to do.

27

THE PROMISE: BECAUSE GOD IS FAITHFUL, YOU MUST NEVER LOSE HOPE

Let us hold fast the confession of our hope without wavering, for He who promised is faithful.

HEBREWS 10:23 NASB

There are few sadder sights on earth than the sight of a man or woman who has lost all hope. In uncertain times, hope can be elusive, but those who place their faith in God's promises need never lose it. After all, God is good; His love endures; and He has promised His children the gift of eternal life.

Despite God's promises, despite Christ's love, and despite our countless blessings, we frail human beings can still lose hope from time to time. When we do, we need the encouragement of Christian friends, the life-changing power of prayer, and the healing truth of God's Holy Word.

If you find yourself falling into the spiritual traps of worry and discouragement, seek the healing touch of Jesus and the encouraging words of fellow believers. And if you find a friend in need, remind him or her of the peace that is found through a personal relationship with Jesus. It was Christ who promised, "These things I have spoken unto you, that in me ye might have peace. In the world ye shall have tribulation: but be of good cheer; I have overcome the world" (John 16:33 KJV). This world can be a place of trials and tribulations, but as believers, we are secure. God has promised us peace, joy, and eternal life. And, of course, God keeps His promises today, tomorrow, and forever.

MORE THOUGHTS ABOUT HOPE

Faith looks back and draws courage; hope
looks ahead and keeps desire alive.

JOHN ELDREDGE

If your hopes are being disappointed just now,
it means that they are being purified.

OSWALD CHAMBERS

The presence of hope in the invincible
sovereignty of God drives out fear.

JOHN PIPER

Down through the centuries in times of trouble and trial, God has brought courage to the hearts of those who love Him. The Bible is filled with assurances of God's help and comfort in every kind of trouble which might cause fears to arise in the human heart. You can look ahead with promise, hope, and joy.

BILLY GRAHAM

Without the certainty of His resurrection, we would come to the end of this life without hope, with nothing to anticipate except despair and doubt. But because He lives, we rejoice, knowing soon we will meet our Savior face to face, and the troubles and trials of this world will be behind us.

BILL BRIGHT

MORE FROM GOD'S WORD

This hope we have as an anchor of the soul,
a hope both sure and steadfast.

HEBREWS 6:19 NASB

I say to myself, "The LORD is mine, so I hope in him."

LAMENTATIONS 3:24 NCV

The LORD is good to those who wait for Him, to the
soul who seeks Him. It is good that one should hope
and wait quietly for the salvation of the LORD.

LAMENTATIONS 3:25–26 NKJV

Hope deferred makes the heart sick.

PROVERBS 13:12 NKJV

Be strong and courageous, all you
who put your hope in the LORD.

PSALM 31:24 HCSB

A TIMELY TIP

If you're experiencing hard times, you'll be wise to start spending more time with God. If you do your part, He will most certainly do his part. So never be afraid to hope—or to ask—for a miracle.

28

THE PROMISE: GOD HAS A PLAN FOR YOU

*But as it is written: What eye did not see and ear did
not hear, and what never entered the human mind—
God prepared this for those who love Him.*

1 CORINTHIANS 2:9 HCSB

Why did God put me here?" It's a simple question to ask and, at times, a very complicated question to answer.

As you seek to discover (or, perhaps, rediscover) God's plan for your life, you should start by remembering this: you are here because God put you here, and He did so for a very good reason—His reason.

At times you may be confident that you are doing God's will. But on other occasions you may be uncertain about the direction that your life should take. At times you may wander aimlessly in a wilderness of your own making. And sometimes you may struggle mightily against God in a vain effort to find success and happiness through your own means, not His. But wherever you find yourself—whether on the mountaintops, in the valleys, or at the crossroads of life—you can be sure that God is there. And you can be sure that He has a plan.

Once you manage to align yourself with God's plan for your life, you will be energized, you will be enthused, and you will be blessed. That's why you should strive to understand what it is that God wants you to do. But how can you know precisely what

God's intentions are? The answer, of course, is that even the most well-intentioned believers face periods of uncertainty and doubt about the direction of their lives. So, too, will you.

When you arrive at one of life's inevitable crossroads, that's the moment when you should turn your thoughts and prayers toward God. When you do, He will make Himself known to you in a time and manner of His choosing. When you discover God's plan for your life, you will experience abundance, peace, joy, and power: God's power. And that's the only kind of power that really matters.

MORE THOUGHTS ABOUT GOD'S PLAN

One of the wonderful things about being a Christian
is the knowledge that God has a plan for our lives.

WARREN WIERSBE

God has no problems, only plans. There
is never panic in heaven.

CORRIE TEN BOOM

Do not let Satan deceive you into being
afraid of God's plans for your life.

R. A. TORREY

God will not permit any troubles to come upon
us unless He has a specific plan by which great
blessing can come out of the difficulty.

PETER MARSHALL

MORE FROM GOD'S WORD

For My thoughts are not your thoughts,
and your ways are not My ways . . . . For as
heaven is higher than earth, so My ways
are higher than your ways, and My
thoughts than your thoughts.

ISAIAH 55:8–9 HCSB

O LORD, you are our Father. We are the clay, and you
are the potter. We are all formed by your hand.

ISAIAH 64:8 NLT

For whoever does the will of God is My
brother and My sister and mother.

MARK 3:35 NKJV

We must do the works of Him who sent Me while it
is day. Night is coming when no one can work.

JOHN 9:4 HCSB

REMEMBER THIS

God has a wonderful plan for your life. And the time to start look-ing for that plan—and living it—is now. Discovering God's plan begins with prayer, but it doesn't end there. You must also do the work that the Lord has placed before you, seeking His guidance day by day, until His intentions become clear to you.

29

THE PROMISE: GOD WANTS YOU TO CELEBRATE LIFE TODAY

This is the day the LORD has made; let us rejoice and be glad in it.

PSALM 118:24 HCSB

The words of John 9:4 remind us that "night is coming" for all of us. But until then, God gives us each day and fills it to the brim with possibilities. Each new day is presented to us fresh and clean at midnight, free of charge, but we must beware: today is a non-renewable resource—once it's gone, it's gone forever. Our responsibility, of course, is to use this day in the service of God's Son and in accordance with His commandments.

Today is a priceless gift that has been given to you by the Creator of the universe—don't waste it. Don't stand on the sidelines as life's parade passes you by. Instead search for the hidden possibilities that the Lord has placed along your path. This day is a one-of-a-kind treasure that can be put to good use . . . or not. Your challenge is to use this day joyfully and productively. And while you're at it, encourage others to do likewise. After all, night is coming when no one can work.

MORE THOUGHTS ABOUT TODAY'S GIFT

How ridiculous to grasp for future gifts
when today's is set before you. Receive
today's gift gratefully, unwrapping it
tenderly and delving into its depths.

SARAH YOUNG

Today is mine. Tomorrow is none of
my business. If I peer anxiously
into the fog of the future, I will strain
my spiritual eyes so that I will not see
clearly what is required of me now.

ELISABETH ELLIOT

Each day is God's gift of a fresh unspoiled
opportunity to live according to His priorities.

ELIZABETH GEORGE

Every day we live is a priceless gift
of God, loaded with possibilities to learn
something new, to gain fresh insights.

DALE EVANS ROGERS

The one word in the spiritual vocabulary is now.

OSWALD CHAMBERS

MORE FROM GOD'S WORD

*But encourage each other every day while it is
"today." Help each other so none of you will become
hardened because sin has tricked you.*

HEBREWS 3:13 NCV

*So don't worry about tomorrow, because tomorrow will have
its own worries. Each day has enough trouble of its own.*

MATTHEW 6:34 NCV

*There is a time for everything, and a season
for every activity under the heavens.*

ECCLESIASTES 3:1 NIV

*The world and its desires pass away, but whoever
does the will of God lives forever.*

1 JOHN 2:17 NIV

*So teach us to number our days, that we may
present to You a heart of wisdom.*

PSALM 90:12 NASB

A TIMELY TIP

Today is a wonderful, one-of-a-kind gift from God. Treat it that
way.

30

THE PROMISE OF ETERNAL LIFE

For God so loved the world, that he gave his only
begotten Son, that whosoever believeth in him
should not perish, but have everlasting life.

JOHN 3:16 KJV

The Bible makes this promise: when you believe in Jesus and give your heart to Him, you will receive an incredible gift: the gift of eternal life. This promise is unambiguous, and it's the cornerstone of the Christian faith.

Jesus is not only the light of the world; He is also its salvation. He came to this earth so that we might not perish but instead spend eternity with Him. What a glorious gift; what a priceless opportunity!

As mere mortals, we cannot fully understand the scope, and thus the value, of eternal life. Our vision is limited, but God's is not. He sees all things; He knows all things; and His plans for you extend throughout eternity.

If you haven't already done so, this moment is the perfect moment to turn your life over to God's only begotten Son. When you give your heart to the Son, you belong to the Father—today, tomorrow, and for all eternity.

MORE THOUGHTS ABOUT ACCEPTING CHRIST

Trust God's Word and His power more
than you trust your own feelings and experiences.
Remember, your Rock is Christ, and it is the sea
that ebbs and flows with the tides, not Him.

LETTIE COWMAN

Blessed assurance, Jesus is mine!
O what a foretaste of glory divine!

FANNY CROSBY

Ultimately, our relationship with Christ is
the one thing we cannot do without.

BETH MOORE

The crucial question for each of us is this:
What do you think of Jesus, and do you yet
have a personal acquaintance with Him?

HANNAH WHITALL SMITH

The destiny of your own soul is in your own
hands by the choice you make.

BILLY GRAHAM

MORE FROM GOD'S WORD

And this is the testimony: God has given us eternal life, and this life is in His Son. The one who has the Son has life. The one who doesn't have the Son of God does not have life.

1 JOHN 5:11–12 HCSB

For the wages of sin is death, but the gift of God is eternal life in Christ Jesus our Lord.

ROMANS 6:23 NIV

If the Spirit of him who raised Jesus from the dead is living in you, he who raised Christ from the dead will also give life to your mortal bodies because of[e] his Spirit who lives in you.

ROMANS 8:11 NLT

Therefore we were buried with Him by baptism into death, in order that, just as Christ was raised from the dead by the glory of the Father, so we too may walk in a new way of life.

ROMANS 6:4 HCSB

I am the good shepherd. The good shepherd lays down his life for the sheep.

JOHN 10:11 NIV

REMEMBER THIS

God offers you the priceless gift of eternal life. If you have not yet accepted His gift, the appropriate moment to do so is now.